HEARTSONG

A Collection of Reflections and Poetry

by

IONA JENKINS

To Nona and Glyn
December 2016
Best Wishes
Iona Jenkins

Copyright © 2016 Iona Jenkins

All rights reserved.

ISBN: 978-1540442833

CONTENTS

The Way	1
Iona	3
Singing Bowl	5
Twilight	9
Rose Gold	11
Awen	13
Five Elements	15
Saint Bride's Blue Magic	17
St. Non's – A Stone's Story	19
Senses	21
Wonder	25
Silver Blue	27
Coastal Sunset	29
Shipwreck	31
Reaching Out	33
The Seagull	35
Bluebells	37
Syon Park	39
Heron	41
Pine Trees	43
Green Valley	45
The River	47
January Reflections	49
Traveller	51
Solitary Thoughts	53

Pathways	55
Alone	57
Winter Solstice	59
Belonging	61
Meditation	63
Peacock	65
Butterfly	67
The Gift	69
Sunny Day	71
Messengers	73
Armadillo	75
Wise Owl	77
Girl From Peru	79
Sikh Wedding	81
Lingua Degli Angeli	83
Capella Sistina	85
Sunflowers, Reflections in Assisi	87
In Tune	91
Orange East To West	93
Safely Gathered In	95
The Autumn Term	97
The Harvest	107
Death Of A Tree	109
Saint Illtud's Church Llantwit Major	111
White Sails	113
Magical Room	115
Heartsong	117
About The Author	119

THE WAY

I felt like I was standing in a painting
I saw a way of words winding and fluid
a meandering meadow stream singing,
ripples playful, sunlit and magic.
I followed on and on, flowing with the current
to a place at the centre of the song where
the path, the stream, the words and I merged
and nothing else was important then.

IONA

Iona, island suspended in time

like I was never anywhere before

and there is nowhere else to go.

SINGING BOWL

I lift the Tibetan singing bowl from its special place in the oak cabinet – I've been meaning to dust those shelves for days. I own three of these bowls, but this one, the smallest, is different because of its age and mysterious origins.

As soon as my fingers close around it, my memory transports me back to a hillside café in Nepal where I once watched the jagged snow peaks of the Himalayas catching fire as the sun set on that New Year's Eve in a blaze of metallic rose and crimson. It was a younger time, a time of freedom, a time without fear, a time of searching, wanting to know.

I haggled for the bowl until I got what seemed to be a fair price. Sitting on a pavement in the small square, I listened to the musical tones of the four bowls for sale, before choosing the one I liked the best, the one which felt comfortable, resonant, like the voice of a good friend.

Later, I take to wondering about its origins; could it have belonged to a Tibetan monk escaping oppression? Had it been lost, stolen or simply sold to pay for food in a life beset by poverty and the hardships of a difficult terrain?

To me, this bowl is a sacred object with an unknown past, a thing of magic, a call to prayer or meditation. Placing it in the palm of my left hand, I strike it with a modern wooden beater bought in Britain but the singing bell metal carries on and on, transporting me far away into the high Himalayas, beautiful and dangerous, spiritual yet inhospitable.

Once the sound dies away, I can examine the bowl's battered uneven surface, touching the places where the yellow metal is grazed and pitted. In a voice of ancient wisdom, it tells me that it has been both scarred and illuminated by life's experiences. It is not in its essence unlike me, which is why I was drawn to it in the first place and why I still love it so much. I tap it again:

"To whom, did you belong?" I ask as it sings to me. "Where have you been? What have you seen?"

And each time I ask, the answer always comes to me in pictures, a vision of mountain goats, a Tibetan tiger rug and the drip, drip of thawing snow from the arch of a rustic wooden door, which is always open.

I stand, immobile, mesmerised by the possibility of an open door within my mind until I decide to throw all caution to the wind and enter.

The dwelling is simple, primitive, pungent and smoky from the burning sticks of incense and butter lamps. The single occupant, an aged monk, cross-legged, with creased parchment skin and eyes as deep as mountain pools has a smile as wide as his face.

"Sit," he says, gesturing to the ground in front of him. "Sit, be still and listen."

I hear the high ringing tone of the singing bowl spreading out in waves of sound as the monk strikes it one time only. As the sound circles around me I listen as instructed.

"Who are you?" asks the monk in the hypnotic sound of the bell.

I hear my own voice try to speak but it sticks in my throat and I cannot say. The bell is struck again and my head begins to spin from the effect of the moving notes and the smell of incense. The question is repeated but I cannot answer.

"Who are you?"

Now the rustic room is gone and I am walking slowly on white sand in a sheltered bay, where the pebbles are pink, green, white and grey. A clump of creamy sheep's wool blows across the emerald grass and amethyst heather into the cool aquamarine of this western ocean.

A Celtic breeze blows through my wild hair as I flow across the sand, which, though it sticks around my toes, is comfortable. The raucous gulls cry freedom and a plump grey seal, sings back to them in the voice of a mermaid. Tales of Faery and Selkie come to life with all their possibilities of music, myth, magic, enchantment and something nameless, which is much bigger than all of this.

"Who are you?" sings the plump grey seal to the ice blue sky and the lapping waves, "who are you?"

"I cannot say," I reply, "but I can tell you that I think I have come home."

I strike the bell one last time before I place it back on the shelf in the oak cabinet. The sound spreads like ripples on the surface of a still lake amidst green mountains. The life in the sound becomes the life in me as it re-awakens a powerful urge to explore new landscapes and listen to words in languages I cannot yet speak. Finding my way home will be easier now.

TWILIGHT

The sound of church bells draws me in.

Wild geese call to the rising moon,

the air is heavy with water

a calm sea washes the shore.

The breeze feels cold

as pink tinged clouds

melt away towards the west

when night begins its approach

at magical twilight,

a door between worlds

or Heaven and Earth.

Can you hear it?

A golden harp is singing.

ROSE GOLD

Azure sunset spaces open
like doors into a mystery.
The new season's colours are
orange and salmon, fuchsia and saffron
circles of smoky violet and grey.
The wonder of twilight
when the street lamps are lit
and the world begins to turn
from bright vibrant day
into, deep soothing night.
Soon there will be stars
and a cool silver moon
to light my slow path home.
A lone pigeon flaps its way
from frozen red rooftop
to brown winter treetop.
There are mystic possibilities
where I stand at the centre
bathed in shining rose gold.

AWEN

When I was a child of four
my home was an enchanted castle.
There were wild flowers in the meadows
and blossoms like pink sugar.
After winter came the scented spring
miraculous, renewed, reborn.

There was no bad news television then
and the world was ripe with magic
like the old clay wizard on my shelf;
starry robed in cobalt blue.
Merlin, elder, man of myth
speaking wisdom down the years.

In field and wood, the lady Olwen
walks before me on the path,
flowers spring as her feet touch the grass.

Then from her lilting silver voice

like the sea's breath on strings of gold,

harmonic words begin to form and resonate,

they dance, they flow, they scintillate

like saffron rays of sunlight

on an ever moving stream.

FIVE ELEMENTS

I am a drop in an ocean

I am a grain of sand

I am a breath of air

I am a spark in a flame

I am a point of conscious existence.

SAINT BRIDE'S BLUE MAGIC

The coastal path

primeval winding snake

mysteries on the edge

breaking waves on rugged cliffs

windswept and pounding.

Gulls float on rafts of air

above St. Bride's bay blue magic

a thinning misty veil

a glimpse of dimensions

and time interrupted,

the birthing stone of legend

hard labour, simple faith

has carved the Celtic cross

where past and present merge,

two streams converging

in the same space, the mother

marble white goddess,

the fertile source bubbles

and bursts flowing

from beneath her feet.

The spring robe of Gaia

daffodil pearl embellished

a pale sun sparkles

on lunar healing water.

The well of St. Non.

ST. NON'S – A STONE'S STORY

A stony story

time travelling

rocky record

pitted, battered chipped

and waterworn

the long lasting bold

building block with

myriad magic memories

of earthwalk and surfcrash

on curving Celtic cliffs

is granite greyed

solid and softly surfaced

in coppery coloured cover

and deftly dipped down

wild woman well.

SENSES

A Walk to Saint Non's

I like to employ intuition in the same proportion as intellect. I've discovered I can slip from the world of logic into a dimension of myth and magic without the slightest effort and then blend the two for a more rounded experience. In my youth, I chose to ignore this aspect of my nature, which I think was born from spending the first four years of my life at my grandparents' home, a smallholding, where I only had the company of other children when my cousins came to visit. Now in more senior years as an elder and writer, I find that allowing this ability creates a richer, fuller dimension, which adds meaning to my life.

Take a walk with me down to St. Non's well and her ruined chapel, an ancient monument in the field beyond. Excuse me a minute will you, whilst I get one Nordic walking pole from the car, since my left ankle isn't as strong as it used to be and the path to the well is rocky and uneven. The metal pole taps against the stones and sinks into the soil, supporting my weight as I move forward. Slow down with me, and feel the earth under your feet, notice how it supports you and how your own ankles feel right now.

Now we are going to employ our senses in this environment, connected to it rather than rapidly passing through, like we're scurrying on a path from birth to death without really noticing the fullness, the myriad facets of our lives in between. Can you feel the dampness in the wind, like a protective mist, cloaking your shoulders, cool but soft as down upon your face? Listen ... can you hear the awesome power of the surf crashing on the rocky coastline of St. Bride's Bay?

We are almost at the well - listen again ... to the sound of water running from beneath the feet of the statue of the Virgin Mary or the Celtic earth goddess Bridget if you prefer that image. I think of the land's lifeblood running through her veins in underground streams.

Contrast this sound with the ocean ... I hear gentle balm, ease and relaxation and can scarcely believe that it's formed from the same element as the sea, one so sweet and the other salt. Listen again to the surf crashing then the spring, gurgling its way through the grass, then close your eyes and breathe deeply, listening to both at the same time. Be still, take in the experience for yourself and add your own impressions. Take your hearing somewhere else, can you listen to the melodic song of the robin, perky and bright in the tree in a flash of scarlet feathers; then the haunting cry of the gull, as contrasting as the spring and the tide, but both are birds, two different aspects of one manifestation.

Now use your eyes. The yellow primroses are creamy, buttery and the yellow daffodils are vibrant, lemony. The stone of the statue is white, carved, but the well cover is an arch built from many grey stones cemented together and solid, unlike the walls of the ruined chapel where the building blocks have separated with time. The spring green grass and ice blue sky add a further touch of colour to the palette, which has formed the masterpiece you are standing in.

Let us open the gate, you first, It creaks and only admits one person at a time. There's a clanging sound, which bites the air behind you as it closes again. Can you taste the salt in the wind and smell the ozone ... the cleanliness of this place? A walker heading in the opposite direction says hello. We have all made an unspoken agreement to be polite and return any greetings from other humans as we head across the field.

Stand outside the next gate leading into the ruined chapel. You may or may not wish to read the plaque before you enter. How do you feel, standing outside looking in? Now walk through the gate into history. How is it now for you surrounded by those ancient walls? Speaking for myself, I would like to say that I am at the centre of something, standing in a creation space open to the elements and perhaps challenging. Notice the birthing stone in the corner. They say St. Non gave birth to St. David on it. What do you want to say? Run a finger around the rough simple Celtic cross carved into its battered surface. Does a sixth sense come into play, a strong feeling or image, or is it just old stone?

Come with me now to the new St. Non's chapel built in the grounds of the retreat house, a place of quiet reflection on your coastal path walk. Although a much more recent construction, the chapel is built with recycled stones from the old one so the magic hasn't been lost. What is it like outside this door? Listen again to the sea and the gulls, the voices of passers-by on the path below the garden. Employ all your senses including your sixth if you can.

When you push the door open, it's stiff and grates a little. Walk through and close it. How does this differ from the outside? Light falls in soft rainbows from the stained glass window filtering through the image of St. Non dressed in cobalt blue, illuminating the altar below it. Prayer candles flicker, in the wrought iron holder before the statue of the Madonna and child. Can you feel the warmth from the flames and hear the silence? The sea and the gulls are shut out, a distant memory in this cloak of sanctuary which floats around your shoulders. Can you feel her protective maternal embrace? Can you spend some time to be nurtured, cared for and loved? Can you also take that with you as you walk the wild path on the edge of jagged cliffs? Have you woven the magic into the reality? Go on ... give it a try ... you might just surprise yourself.

WONDER

Breathing deep of the air and the sky

the roar and the sigh of the incoming tide

embrace and entrance me like music and magic.

I am filled with life, with joy, with wonder

like a child in the sunlit morning

when the world is perfect.

SILVER BLUE

The lamp of early sunlight on a pale ocean

the gush and gurgle of waves and the soft white foam,

sigh and flow on this pastel morning painting

an eternal pounding sound of becoming

the light is brighter than my eyes can focus

and the sea stretches out into silver blue infinity.

Drifting aware into the bliss of this connection

I am nowhere, I am here I am everywhere

in the tide washed rocks, in the damp sandy grains

in the swirling music of the surging summer sea.

COASTAL SUNSET

The silver blue sea to the East

is rose tinted to the West.

Salmon pink clouds mingled with grey

float across the last remaining blue

of fading day-time sky

two islands in an ocean of copper ripples

lit by deeply drowning rays

from a dreaming sunset.

This hour of contemplation

the dusky watery landscape

which floats outside my window.

This hour ripe with promise

of doorways and dimensions.

Soon the day will be spent

as twinkling lights on the opposite shore

gaze deep at their reflections

in an ocean of night.

SHIPWRECK

A fragile boat, a hostile sea

white spray hurled

at battered granite;

I will never forget your letter

on that cold January day.

I looked out at the snow

upon the evergreens

and thought about the storm;

the mess of wreckage on the beach

our time together broken on the sand.

REACHING OUT

Wherever you may be

I shall always love you.

From wherever I am

I shall steal across the bounds of time

to sit quietly beside you

when you are alone or sick

afraid or sad.

When the fading jaded sunshine

of this rapid spinning world

has turned your green leaves gold

and autumn's chilly breeze

blows cold upon your face

so shall midsummer, healing warmth

contained within my lightest touch

with soft caresses linger on your brow

and the sweetest, deepest music of my soul

shall sing you to sleep.

THE SEAGULL

Soaring aloft on winds of change

the white seagull pleases itself.

Diving into ocean rollers

unfettered and free

awakes deep longing in my heart

to break the heavy chains of pain

I have on days of darkness forged myself

and then to follow in its freedom flight

over bright light cliffs and clear blue seas.

BLUEBELLS

I caught the heady scent

of bluebells in the glade

and knew I was alive when

I saw the colour of heaven

shining in the sunlight.

SYON PARK

Even in the hot daylight

I sense the moon's reflection

in the still silent lake of Syon.

Across the water sits an artist

who is sketching as I write.

The scent of white lilies

follows me when I leave.

HERON

The heron guards the entrance

to the magic place

the sky and treetops

deep reflections in the lake

suggest a cool green doorway

the entrance to another world.

PINE TREES

The wind, playing in the Scots pines

a song of heaven on a harp

the woody perfume of ripened cones

a tree top censor of sacred resin

My mind is stilled, my senses warmed.

GREEN VALLEY

The bubbling cauldron river

a wall of trees along the bank

fields are unfolding like green blankets

black mountain peaks touch the sky

white clouds rain down like doves.

THE RIVER

The river on its smooth course flowing

pays no heed to rushes growing on its banks

or rocks and silt that block its way

I watch it rise to laugh and play

till all those things are worn away.

If safe would reach my journey's end

like reed in wind must learn to bend

or like the river learn to flow

where destiny would have me go.

JANUARY REFLECTIONS

Still water like a winter mirror

reflects the dove grey sky above

the smallest hint of sunlight

creates a tiny golden thread of warmth

the shrill clear calls of seabirds

invade the streams of misty air

like a loud radio piercing my thoughts.

TRAVELLER

The bright white stars hang like lanterns

in this winter solstice sky.

They invite me to follow their light

and call to me in notes of magic music

from the deepest caverns of my heart

with sound so pure and clear that soon,

my head begins to whirl, responding to their song.

And so imprisoned far too much

within my mortal logic brain

I'd chart a course to set my spirit's love in flight

across the universe or even far beyond

to free adventure's magic dancing child

who yearns to cross the frontiers of creation.

SOLITARY THOUGHTS

In the winter of my life
I shall not be afraid
after winter comes the spring
a time of joy and rebirth.

Sometimes, beautiful things
are born in desperate places.

This deep ocean of sorrow
makes me want to write my heart out.

In accepting the loss of things
I did not or could not choose
I find my freedom.

An ending and a beginning
are just opposite sides
of the same doorway.

In the company of true friends
I never feel old.

Wisdom lives but not too hard
Wisdom works but not too hard
Wisdom plays but not too hard
Wisdom tries but not too hard
Too hard is not usually so wise
It's only exhausting.

PATHWAYS

Old paths lead into new ways
and each one has its share of
joy, pain and chance encounters.
Listen to your heartbeat in every moment
now is the secret of happiness.

No one really wins or loses
choose your path
and follow it to the end
or choose again at every crossroads.

If only you knew
how much you are loved
you would never be sad.
At this moment and always
Heaven is celebrating your life.

ALONE

I celebrate the fact

that I am alone

I let go of wanting

to be with others;

That is not here

that is not now.

Understanding this moment

I find my freedom

in the full experience

of this alone time

under the trees.

WINTER SOLSTICE

The berries, red as flowing blood

cascade and tumble down

amongst the deepest green

of holly tree and yew.

A robin perches on a branch

his scarlet breast ablaze

with warm December passion.

After the sorrow comes resurrection

after the winter floral shooting spring

will paint the world in scented light.

BELONGING

I belong in this gentle garden green
so far away from crowing crowds.
The song of the soaring summer lark
renews my spirits, entrances my mind.
The light as air nut gathering squirrels
flow along the branches of tall trees
balancing evergreen tight-rope walkers
with no fear of falling they sail on a breeze
light of limb and lighter still of heart
they remind me that I am also just myself
and that is good enough.

MEDITATION

Sometimes, on free Saturday afternoons in London, I would go walking and find a suitable bench beneath the trees in one of the wilder parts of Kew Gardens. I used to enjoy short meditations in this creative green space; it was a chance to calm my speedy, chattering mind, to experience connection and communion.

Then, one day after such a meditation, I opened my eyes to discover the surprise presence of a peahen, lying peacefully at my feet like a silent, watchful companion. I remained still and focussed but she did not move, instead she closed her eyes and slept or maybe she had found her own communion.

I sat with her whilst she slept and when she opened her eyes I thanked her for her company and continued on my way. Why did she come to me? Perhaps she was a guide on my journey, a guardian to watch over me during meditation, or perhaps she was simply attracted by the peace, which happens when the mind is stilled.

PEACOCK

Lazily the strutting peacock

makes his way around the pond

flashing feathers of emerald and sapphire

he does not mind the weekend people

he remains contentedly peacock.

BUTTERFLY

Those who in their search for truth

would self-improvement choose

must not forget at any cost

when courage fails and all seems lost

that each bright jewelled butterfly

in coloured splendour flashing by

began existence as a worm.

THE GIFT

A butterfly
am I am I
I flower flit
I fly and fly.

On petals bright
I can alight
my silken wings
look best in flight.

In coloured light
I am defined
a blessed gift
to humankind.

My life is brief
my tale soon told
in just two days
I've aged, I'm old.

So soon to fall

on summer earth

a life too short

from time of birth.

A butterfly

Am I am I

please notice me

before I die.

SUNNY DAY

Sigh, sigh, sigh swirls the sound of the breeze

spinning airy spirals as it snakes through the trees.

A gull floats by crac crac, cree cree

a raft of white feathers, high above the sea.

Oi Oi Oi! shouts a black raucous crow

officiously strutting on the grass down below.

Wash, wash, shore … the tidal surge is small

insufficient sound waves to drown the seabirds' call.

A row of white sails glide smoothly away.

The coastline is busy on a hot sunny day.

MESSENGERS

The first time I really noticed the presence of robins in my life was in January 2004.

One bright frosty winter's day, I went walking in Kew Gardens, that magical place I used to frequent once or twice a week during my time in London because it always offered a peaceful sanctuary amidst the bustle of my working life in the Capital.

At this time, my father was ill and my parents had moved from Yorkshire to Lincolnshire in order to be close to my brother and his wife. I began to drive up there more frequently for weekends, trying to balance the visits between my work responsibilities and my own home life.

Although this period was both sad and stressful, the time I spent with my father was precious because I knew he was nearing the end of his life.

On this particular January day, after a brisk walk, I had sat down to rest on one of the many memorial benches, when a fearless robin alighted on the wooden arm- rest inches away from me. There was no song or chirping as the bird bobbed its tiny bright eyed head at me, but words were forming in my own mind, a simple message. "Your father will be gone in the fullness of the Spring Equinox." I stared at the bird and it bobbed its head one more time before flying off into the bushes.

I returned home and thought no more about it until the end of the first week in March when my father was rushed into hospital. He was unconscious with kidney failure and the doctors were advising us against resuscitation because of his already poor quality of life.

My father, however, being an old warrior, did regain consciousness and lived for a further two weeks until every member of the family had visited him to say goodbye. I received the phone call to say he had died just after one a.m. on the 22nd March, which I would describe as being in the fullness of the Spring Equinox. He had lived through the first day of spring, which he had always thought was a special time. Did the robin really bring me a message or did focussing on the bird link me into some kind of inner knowing? It's hard to tell, but I do know that I experience great clarity outside in the natural world.

We put his ashes in a place he used to love when he was a child. Then, as we turned to leave, a skylark flew over us singing a sweet fanfare. I like to think that it came to announce his departure from a challenging life and to sing to him on his journey.

After that, two robins took up residence in my garden but there were no other messages.

ARMADILLO

One evening on holiday in Florida, I was fortunate enough to experience a very close encounter with an armadillo. Returning home after an evening meal, I saw the creature on the lawn in front of the house where I was staying.

Never having met an armadillo before, and because it was such a strange looking creature, I made the decision to investigate it further. I stood very still observing the animal foraging in the grass, before beginning to stroke its armoured little back. It felt like hard plastic.

After allowing the intrusion for a few seconds, the armadillo pulled its nose out of the lawn and looked at me with its bright little eyes. It must have decided that I was harmless because after studying me for a few seconds with turning ears, it returned to foraging in the grass. I continued the stroking but was ignored until it decided to look for a new place to eat. The nose came out of the lawn and the little face lifted to look at me again before the creature turned away and trotted off towards a neighbouring lawn.

An American friend said that it was impossible to stroke armadillos because they always run away when approached by humans. Maybe my armadillo was quite a tame one, used to people or maybe it just liked me. Sometimes I just feel privileged to live in a world, which has so many amazing creatures living alongside us humans.

WISE OWL

Old wise owl, she lives in the west,

she's learned a lot from her life.

There has been sorrow and joy,

difficulty and ease, sickness and health

adventure and a time to rest,

new beginnings, both sad and happy endings,

times of birth and of death and mourning.

She knows too well that all things change.

Beautiful things come into being

they thrive for a while

then wither and die

leaving space for the new to emerge.

It's part of the dance, whatever we feel,

though it's often hard to understand.

Old wise owl stands by the wheel of life

which turns with or without her.

Gives love, receives love, when she can

encounters hate or indifference sometimes

but tries hard not to return it.

Let go, move on when love has gone.

She knows the score, she's seen it all before.

GIRL FROM PERU

Tame and wild

Moonlight child

in the shallowness of life

you did not notice your depths

that is, until now.

The treasure is gradually revealed

as each new day, the chest

opens up just a little more.

Inside, there is art and poetry,

wild places with animals and

cultured places with historic architecture;

stories of great romance and daring

magic, adventure, visionary quests,

fables of Spain and Native America,

the jewels you find at top of the chest.

But one day, you will discover them all

And then you'll be filled with wonder.

SIKH WEDDING

The guests are all sweetened

with silvered confection.

Swarthy and turbaned

the drummers take the stage,

yellow brocaded like princes

the festive drums on leather straps

are balanced on their chests,

intricate symmetrical designs

like henna on the bride's hands.

As the skins are struck

rhythmic and loud, resonant, primal

a coloured sari silken sea

feet stamping, hips swaying

hands snaking, jewelled fingers flashing

hot as stars in an Indian summer.

Dreamy and drugged by the beat

my heart moves my blood

like the drum moves the dance.

LINGUA DEGLI ANGELI (The Language of Angels)

There's peace in dove grey mountains

and this rich red Roman earth

as late October sunshine wraps my skin

in the scent of ripened lemons.

When the leaves turn just a little gold,

I see the inspiration like a lighted lamp

and my mind becoming still at last

is more than just a little glad to be here.

Italy is a warm embracing place

where my own creative truth out runs

the waves of restless racing thoughts

and the sound of my heart's voice rises,

singing songs in the language of angels.

CAPELLA SISTINA (Sistine Chapel)

We walk a long sacred way like pilgrims, in corridors of cobalt blue and starry skies, to the entrance of the Sistine Chapel. The doorway opens into the otherworld of someone else's fantastic imagination. Above my head, the genius of Michelangelo, whose bright palette created magic from a rainbow, where the figures look three-dimensional like tiny living people hanging from the ceiling and where, at the centre, the hand of God reaches out to touch Adam.

The crowds are staring awed and excited, they talk and talk in the space below the magic.

"Silenzio!"

The voice of the uniformed guard is deep, resonant, booming above the endless chatter and analysis of artistic genius; that divine inspired madness, which cannot be explained. The sound stops in obedience but begins again in seconds. Perhaps in silence the whole thing might seem just too powerful … for some.

In the space between the silence and the sound I sense the profound holiness of a place where heaven and earth meet in an artist's brush strokes, a place hallowed by centuries of ritual and prayer, the conclave where each new Pope is chosen.

I make my way towards an empty seat to find my own sacred space amidst the endless stream of visitors. I should like to be alone here to breathe in colour and incense.

SUNFLOWERS

REFLECTIONS IN ASSISI

Girasole - How well the Italian word evokes the essence of the flower. Today in Assisi the heat from the sun feels like sunflowers, gentle and penetrating, soft, bright and happy. My joints feel nurtured, my knees and shoulders are cheerful and flexible. In May, the Italian countryside is abundantly green, lush with wildflowers and trees laden with lemons. Olive groves line the hillside with a promise of harvest, a promise of extra virgin oil.

Assisi, clean stone and mediaeval, perched upon the slopes of Mount Subasio. It is busy and sacred, relaxed and ancient. There are pilgrims and tourists seeking to trace the footsteps of San Francesco, a thirteenth century revolutionary who became a monk and made the church available to the whole population instead of just the wealthy.

What was it he felt nearly eight centuries ago and why did so many young people in this town follow his example? At this moment, I resist the temptation to buy a book from one of the many shops selling statues, plaques and other religious paraphernalia. I am seeking the inspiration, the spirit of Francesco Bernadone not the history or the hearsay.

I have some success in the sanctuary of San Damiano. This is the first church in the area to be restored by the saint. Walking outside the city walls he found it in ruin, except for the presence of a Byzantine cross, a presence Francesco found inspiring.

"Restore my church!" said a voice from the cross. And Francesco did just that, following his inspiration until it was complete, putting all his energy and life into this one task like an artist painting a masterpiece or a musician producing a great concerto.

What do I feel sitting on a pew in this old stone, looking at the newer Byzantine cross and then beyond it towards an evocative wall painting of the Madonna depicted in softest green, blue, ochre and terracotta. The footsteps of twenty first century pilgrims echo on the flagstones as they have for centuries but for all that, a holy silence fills the cool dark interior of this first simple church, which seems in my mind to merge with the landscape outside. Is this how Francesco was able to trust in the abundance of God to sustain him? Is this how he was able to give up his comfortable life to follow his divine inspiration, his dream his passion? Some of the town elders said he was mad but the young did not.

Later in the Piazza del Comune, I discover a different kind of church, or at least that is what I first thought. The façade is Roman with an age of over two thousand years. I touch the pillars with a sense of wonder. How many people has this stone witnessed? I have to admit that I am a little overawed as my mind struggles with the concept of so many births, lives and deaths.

The interior is cool, decorated in typical lavish Catholic tradition more reminiscent of Dolce and Gabbana. A single statue of the Madonna crowned with a halo of electric stars, stands above the altar pouring blessings upon a modern congregation. This place was once the Temple of Minerva before a virgin ever gave birth to a Christ. There has always been something special here. The presence in Assisi seems feminine, inclusive, abundant, protective and creative. There is no wonder that to me the essence of San Francesco feels like sunflowers. Brother Sun is gentle, inspired, inspiring, in spirit, Spiritus Sanctus, Holy Spirit.

From the main square, I locate the Basilica of Santa Chiara – St. Clare, a young woman who also renounced her noble background to work and pray with Francesco. The original Byzantine cross of San Damiano has been removed here with her remains. In the spirit of the Madonna, she cared for the nuns, the population and Francesco when he developed stigmata towards the end of his life. She is out there in the warm stone, on the green hillsides, in the abundant gardens and olive groves. She is definitely not residing in the tomb.

I am surprised and pleased to find the main Basilica of San Francesco open at nine on Saturday evening. The crowds have returned to their hotels for dinner and at last I become immersed in the beauty of the frescoes on the walls and vaulted ceilings. In the crypt, the remains of the Saint lie in state, candle lit and silent. The air is heavy with prayer and supplication. This is a place to focus, give thanks or ask for guidance.

This atmosphere, created, by people over centuries, conjures up the Saint's presence with simple faith, but

Francesco is not really here. I think he is on the hillsides with Santa Chiara, in the olive groves, the flower meadows and the gardens. You can find his spirit in the stones, in the pavements, the sun, the moon, the stars, in ordinary homes and the kindness of people. The curtain between heaven and earth is thin here under the Umbrian sunshine, which makes the round of daily life seem sacred and creative. I feel an urge to write again. Tomorrow as usual, I will awake to the sound of church bells.

IN TUNE

The clicking rhythm of cicadas
dance a languid daydream space
in the drowsy dusty leaf shade
of one straight tree on the square.
I am alone, slowing like a snail
in tune with the hot afternoon
and the natural pace of the place
I am being not doing
I am dreaming not planning
I am silent not talking.

ORANGE EAST TO WEST

For me orange in the East is like India, that spectacular sunrise over the Ganges, which flows through Varanasi, sacred abode of Lord Siva. It's the flames of the funeral pyres from which the ashes of the dead are scattered into the sacred water.

At dawn, pilgrims perform their ablutions pouring the life-blood of Mother Ganges over their heads, oblivious to ash or floating lotus candles. It's a meeting place between life and death or heaven and earth.

The magic happens as the orange ball of sun begins to rise and like an alchemist, turns the water into a river of gold. The town awakens as the wallahs yawn and rise from sleep on their rickshaws to catch the early morning custom.

This orange sunrise is the silk of saris and turbans, garlands of marigolds in the temples and shrines. Orange is the colour of life in this eastern land; it is energetic, noisy, joyful like bhangra drums and the God Nataraja twirling in his circle of flames. His dancing is becoming, living, dying and becoming again in the wheel of life, turning and turning, because energy cannot be destroyed like flesh.

Orange is tigers, butterflies, wonderful spices, fire opals and carnelian lilies inlaid in white marble. My heart loves this exploding life and lively people but something in my physical structure is not resonant in this joyful land of fire and its orange is sometimes too strong for my western body. The demanding Gods issue their challenge to grow and the unfamiliar teeming microbes are an unseen life force, which saps my own. There is both physical and spiritual fire here, heat and purification.

In the West, orange seems cooled by water, mellow and moist. It's the colour of autumn, the harvest, the tint of earthy abundance in the cycle of growth.

The sun rises from the autumnal mist, painting the treetops orange. It shines through the dying leaves creating a treasure chest of amber jewels, which fall to earth in crunching piles of fun for children to play in. Orange is foxes, red squirrels, conkers, beech and hazelnuts, roe deer, leaping salmon, rosehips, Halloween candles and pumpkins.

The orange I would choose to wear now that my hair has silvered, is a paler, apricot or peach. In my youth, I once made a dress of fiery orange with psychedelic swirls like a lava lamp. I would look lost in that now, burned up, consumed, upstaged by its tone. It's a colour, which suits young people and mirrors their high energy levels.

Orange is a wonderful colour; it's cheeky, cheerful, vital, and after all, don't we all want to feel alive and happy? Getting into orange might have some influence on life force and lifespan because there's something immortal about it.

SAFELY GATHERED IN

Wheaten bullion, natures treasure

stacked and gleaming like gold bars

in the afterglow of the sunset

and a hard days field labour.

Roasting like hogs in an August oven.

the farmers are brown beaten copper

skin dry as ripened wheat sheaves

they themselves are warm earth, nurtured.

This year Gaia's loyal land children

all safely gathered in with the harvest

are trudging home languid and weary

to slam the door on Winter's hungry wolf.

THE AUTUMN TERM (A reflection from childhood)

It's the first week in September. The temperature is now somewhere in the mid to late teens and the sun is glaring bright, highlighting the blood red of abundant rowan berries at the edge of the small copse close to the crossroads.

I take a detour from the pavement on to the path through the trees in search of fallen acorns and brown beech- nuts. It is the same ritual every year. The boys collect conkers in prickly cases from around the horse chestnut trees whilst the girls find and share their oak and beech fruit jewels to create necklaces and bracelets fit for princesses. It all costs nothing, but to us, it is ripe treasure trove provided by nature in the harvest time.

I know exactly where the trees are along the path because I have been shown these secrets by my mother at the age of four. I know all the names of all the trees, the local animals and birds, as well as the flowers when they are in bloom. Now it is autumn and the magic is different from July when school broke up for the summer. I am awake to the possibilities of the new season.

Coming out of the copse with my pockets full of riches, I cross the road and walk towards the village in the new black school shoes with leather soles my father has covered with rubber to prevent slipping.

Because this is the beginning of my last year at Primary School, I know that I am going to be in form four. This final class is presided over by the formidable Miss M, spinster of the parish, member of the church committee and renowned tyrant. Her rules are strict and I know that I will get the ruler if I am a nuisance so I am always well behaved and polite.

Miss M. does have some redeeming features though, and one of them is the orchard behind her cottage opposite the church. In the autumn term, she brings some of her apples to the nature lesson, showing us how to cut them to reveal the tiny pips nestling in the natural geometry of a five- pointed star. After learning about the apples, we eat them and that is a real treat because eating anything in lessons is usually totally forbidden.

I love the way that village life follows the seasons in a natural flow of creative energy. Situated south of Leeds we are both a mining and farming community. Hymns in assembly are seasonal rituals.

"We plough the fields and scatter the good seed on the Land …"

Or,

"Come ye thankful people come, raise the song of harvest home …"

Strangely, there are never any hymns about digging up coal. My seven-year old mind wanted an explanation for this but my eleven- year old mind doesn't care because it is more interested in the fields.

I am made a prefect because I am considered to be both smart and reliable. Along with this comes the duty of Ink Monitor. Every morning, I take the jug of watered down blue ink from the big wooden cupboard next to the stove and fill up the pottery inkwells located at the top of every desk. Next I place a small piece of pink blotting paper neatly on each desk lid. Now everybody is ready to learn the new skill of joined up writing, which Miss M. demonstrates on the tall swivel blackboard at the front of the room and which we attempt to copy with our dip in pens.

The nibs scratch across the paper as we concentrate on forming the letters trying not to make blots. Learning to form this script is a rite of passage, which will distinguish us as more grown up than the other years, as well as preparing us for next year's entry into Secondary School life.

When I think about leaving this wonderful little school, an oasis of orderly calm, steeped in village tradition and close to nature, I am wistful and just a little afraid until Miss M. rings the brass hand-bell to announce the morning break. I run out into the Girls' playground to practise handstands and play two-ball. For now, outside in the fresh autumn air, I am still a child.

At the end of September, my father begins to light the coal fire in the kitchen before he goes off to the pit. My mother will light the one in the living room just before we get back from school. There are blue Michaelmas daisies growing in the back garden and the trees are beginning to put on their autumn colours. In a couple of weeks, the world will be changed into a blaze of orange and gold. I love the sight of the sunlight shining through the russet colours of the dying leaves as the trees prepare to shed their foliage for the winter.

As the autumn comes into full swing, the hymns in our school assembly are changed. We now have:

Ye Holy Angels Bright

Fight the Good Fight

He Who Would Valiant Be and

For All the Saints

For Halloween we do not have pumpkins or Trick or Treat on our estate. Instead, some of the children like to make turnip lanterns. This is possibly due to the proximity of a large turnip field, which most dads have to pass on their way home from the pit. The inside is scooped out for cooking before cutting the narrow eyes and a grinning mouth into the turnip. Then, a suitable round space is hollowed out inside the lantern to add an ordinary household candle, fixed in place by dripping the wax. It is always satisfying for us to see the lanterns lit, even if they are not very scary.

Then comes Bonfire Night.

"Remember, remember, the 5th of November,

Gunpowder treason and plot."

Every year, the story is told in school, becoming more factual and sophisticated as we get older. This year, it is a definite history lesson.

I go out chumping with Jane from next door, because we are having our bonfire together. My little brother stays at home because he is still too young. Luckily there are several small woods within a twenty minute walk of our house and there is always a profusion of dead branches to drag back to the garden where my dad will build a fire. My mother has been saving old clothes to make a Guy Fawkes. She sews him together with large tacking stitches ready for the 5th November.

My great aunt Laura turns her talents from Yorkshire puddings to prolific bonfire treats, which we love even though they are sometimes spectacularly unsuccessful. The sticky, golden brown treacle toffee does not always set so it sticks to our teeth. It is no wonder that the fillings I have, all happened before I was 21. The ginger parkin, which is moist but just a little too gingery, is always eaten enthusiastically until the whole batch is finished because we never waste food.

After all the anticipation and hard work, the 5th of November arrives and all the children are excited. We have managed to stop some neighbouring boys from stealing our wood on Mischief Night so our fire is ready to be lit at the end of the garden. After the dog and cat are shut into the front room with the curtains closed, we all go out into the garden with the wonderful fireworks, mostly bought by grandparents. There are two boxes at two shillings and sixpence and a five-shilling box as well as some loose rockets. With the addition of a similar supply of fireworks from next door, we can have a really great celebration.

Only dads are permitted to light the blue touch paper and we all have to stand well back as the instructions say. Guy Fawkes burns on the bonfire for plotting against King James as we pass round aunt Laura's sticky sweet treats. I never like the bangers and jumping crackers but love the starry glory of the roman candles and coloured fire-bursts from the squealing rockets. The Catherine wheels never spin on the wooden washing post and we are all a little disappointed even though it is predictable.

My mother rounds up the evening with hot cups of tea and the merriment goes on until nine when we are all ushered inside to get ready for bed before the fathers do their disappearing act to the Miners' Welfare.

As we move through November, the nights, foggy from the coal fire smoke begin to draw in. The remainder of the gold and amber leaves fall quickly now, leaving the stark, dark branches pointing at the chilly sky. We no longer leap about in the discarded bright, tree finery because it has become soggy, brown and slippery. We are now cosily wrapped in winter woollies. There are hand knitted sweaters and knee length socks produced once again by the enthusiasm of my great aunt, who having no husband or family of her own chooses to lavish her domestication on us. I sometimes wonder what we would do without her.

The old iron stove in the classroom is fed with coal from a lead coloured scuttle. When the snow comes, we all hang our wet socks on the fireguard and watch the steam rise towards the ceiling. I have new ankle boots from Leeds Market, which just like my last pair are black suede with white fur linings and zips up the front.

At the beginning of December, the choir begins rehearsals for the Carol Concert to be held in the village hall with the local doctor as the principal guest. I am very fortunate to be asked to sing in it again because I love the atmosphere we create with Little Donkey, Mary's Boy Child and the Holly and the Ivy. We like to laugh at Miss M. who is waving her arms around as she conducts the music with a fierce expression and such pride. In spite of the secret, conspiratorial laughter, we are really very fond of her and we know that she has the respect of the whole village.

Hymns in assembly are now replaced with carols:

Ding Dong Merrily

Hark the Herald Angels Sing

Once in Royal

Away in a Manger and

While Shepherds watched.

We take great delight in changing the words to make the shepherds wash socks instead of watch flocks. It's all a bit silly but we love it because we are kids and kids like corny jokes.

I find a good place to get holly with berries on the way home from school. I find it tucked away in a clump of bushes next to the Labour MP's house. He doesn't own it, so I take a few twigs for decoration because that will save my mum a bit of money in the market. I love the contrast of the forest green spikes and the pillar- box red berries. There is something holy about it, which makes me think of the crib in church.

In the last few days before Christmas, my great aunt Laura joins forces with my grandmother to produce more Christmas fare than you can get in a bakery. There are mince pies, raspberry jam tarts, lemon curd and small Bakewell tarts. The mouth-watering smell forces us to beg for the pre-festive samples which my grandmother can never refuse. The Christmas cakes are already in the cellar on the stone table. Produced early in November, they have been consigned to tins with an apple to keep them moist. The tarts aligned on trays and covered with greaseproof paper are now next to the cake tins.

We have already decked the tree in our own house with treasures from a box, which sits on the top of my mother's wardrobe. They are cherished like old friends: the Santa with the snowy beard, the rainbow wassail cups, the frosted lanterns, the silver and gold bells and, of course, the golden angel for the tree-top.

On Christmas Eve, my little brother goes to bed early listening for sleigh bells and I stay up to watch TV with my great aunt who is staying with us to babysit whilst my parents join the festivities at the Miners' Welfare.

On Christmas day, I put on my main present, which is a red woollen dress and black velvet beaded pumps. We eat bread and potted meat, a kind of homemade poor man's pate only made at Christmas, before walking to my grand parents' house in the next village. Today is a feast day and thanks to the kindness of relatives and friends we are always able to keep Christmas well.

In the afternoon after the Christmas goose, people call in for a sherry throughout the day, bringing their festive greetings and gifts of silver sixpences, shillings and sometimes, even half crowns for me, and my brother. I remember a time of warmth, friendliness, good food and happy seasonal wishes.

After the new- year, which we celebrate with some of our Scottish neighbours, I turn my thoughts towards the spring. Already new life is growing under the earth beneath my feet as I eagerly await the arrival of the snowdrops, and coltsfoot. When the time comes, I will know exactly where to find them all. The festivals, which are always celebrated in the local church and in my primary school, mark significant places on the turning wheel of the village year and one season follows another as surely as the sun rises.

THE HARVEST

In rolling golden glory

the ripened corn extends before me

sun kissed field of burnished wheat

ebbs and flows around my feet

beneath a dazzling harvest sun

like mingling rippling tides on gilded seas

I hear it on the passing breeze.

"I will provide for you."

DEATH OF A TREE

In its descent, the tree had fallen across the wall into the graveyard behind the church as if to acknowledge its own passing from life into death. It was a magnificent spruce, a toppled giant with green needles still showing a connection to life amidst the cracked bark of its smashed branches.

I stood a while to mourn this giant's passing, asking for a blessing for the spirit of the tree. I gave thanks on behalf of the birds for the shelter it had provided and also for the small part it had played in the eco-system of the local environment then I whispered goodbye and left.

Turning towards life again, I continued and chanced to pass a young man who had suntanned skin and a mass of dark hair, walking two dogs. He greeted me with a warm open smile and a friendly hello, which seemed to come from a place of beauty and I returned the greeting in recognition of a gentle friendly soul.

Sometimes, on a short simple walk around the church, interesting things can happen. As I head back, I feel in harmony with the song of the summer wind echoing across the ocean towards my home and my own life is good.

SAINT ILLTUD'S CHURCH LLANTWIT MAJOR

Saint Illtuds Church with its square tower is built from beautiful grey stone, weathered by time and soft in the bright sunlight of a warm May afternoon. John Wesley preaching here on the 25th July 1777, described it as the most beautiful church in Wales and on a day like this, it's quite easy to see why he loved it so much.

Leaving the sun behind, I enter into the West church through its Norman arch, an old doorway leading me back in time. I am alone in the building and the silence which begins to cloak me in its protective fabric has a life all of its own.

The Celtic crosses which stand in the newly restored Galilee chapel are so much older than I will ever be, older than all the generations of my family that I know about. This awesome fact is difficult for my finite mind to grasp and I wonder how many generations will pass before these old stones crumble into dust and are swept away. Only one of the crosses is completely whole because it has been repaired whilst the tops are missing from the others.

Touching the ancient stone and tracing the Celtic knot work markings with my finger, I can feel a sense of connection down the centuries. There is a sense of mortality and eternity, a sense of wonder. We could be kinder, laugh more and celebrate our lives in the time allotted.

The stone lives on, bearing witness to both joy and struggle for generation after generation; it is cool to the touch, slow and unhurried. I relax as I let go and move through the doors towards the newer east church.

Restored paintings decorate the thick white washed walls. They are beautiful in their simplicity and I love their imperfections and natural colours. I sit in a plain solid oak pew with brilliant modern tapestry cushions and face the altar with its crucifixion carving above an arch.

The air is totally still; the atmosphere, not quite of this century is quiet and soothing. It is easy to slip back in time as I notice a wall painting which says God save King James 1604. I allow my imagination cross the boundaries of time and space until ... I hear voices behind me and there are new visitors entering the sanctuary. The magic is broken and it is time to cross back through the Norman arch into my own time.

WHITE SAILS

I counted twenty white sails

luminous in afternoon sunshine

graceful and slow

on a silver blue sea

calm and smooth as glass

Often if I paint the ocean

I place white sails upon it

somehow that feels complete.

MAGICAL ROOM

What I love about this room is the light pouring in through its dual aspect windows, which both overlook the sea.

The walls and ceiling are painted white to make the most of the room's bright position and the furnishings, which give the impression of a coffee with cream, add a touch of earth and warmth. The light oak cabinets and the carvings on the wall put natural wood into the green and pink flower garden created by the curtains and the cushions scattered on to two leather sofas and a single armchair.

But then there is always the light. Bright rippling sunlight on the morning tide, dazzling and energising, rushing headlong into the room like an eager child, or intermittent, only bursting through at intervals, in pale buttery rays whenever the wind forces the clouds to step aside.

On full moon nights, the sea, now shot with silver light, creates a dreaming pathway right across to Somerset. And later come the rising stars covering the sky at midnight with winking diamond dots as though they had been thrown at random on to a cloth of indigo.

Sometimes when I open the door and step outside on to the balcony, I am caught up in the magic with my senses spinning and my imagination running riot. At other times the sky is ebony like empty space as the deep peace of night at dark of the moon covers the murmuring sea like a raven's wing.

When the sun rises in the east, you can sometimes see a very long way and then the new born light spills across the heavens and through the windows like a bolt of gold and crimson silk ... and everywhere the voices of eager gulls above the waves in search of breakfast fish.

As the sun begins its journey across the sky from east to west, it illuminates the ripples on the sea like a million jewels, which spin around the white walls through the glitter ball like prism of a mirrored silver lamp. I swear that in the whole of my life, I have never lived in any room as magical as this one.

HEARTSONG

The path stretches far and away

from the door I have opened.

I will teach my head to understand

and my feet to dance upon it

For this is the right way to go now.

Sing me the song of my life, my heart

So I can listen and follow you.

ABOUT THE AUTHOR

Iona Jenkins worked as a teacher before changing career to become a counsellor/psychotherapist, mentor and life coach with both young people and adults in London. Her love of nature developed during her own imaginative childhood in a Yorkshire village. Growing up in a mining family, the young Iona loved exploring, discovering special places in all seasons and finding new creative ideas amongst the woods, fields, streams and even colliery wasteland in the countryside around her home. Today, Iona lives and writes amongst the magical landscapes of Wales.

In 2016, Iona published her debut book, The Unicorn Gate, the first of the Legends of Lumenor series of children's fiction. The second instalment is due out in 2017.

www.ionajenkins.com

Printed in Great Britain
by Amazon